How To Stop Feeling Like Shit

WAKE UP YOUR IDEA!

You Know What You Need To Do Right This Minute!

MARC CANNON

Table of Contents

Chapter 1: What Is The Meaning of Life? 6

Chapter 2: The Chosen Ones Choose Themselves 8

Chapter 3: How To Accept Yourself No Matter What 10

Chapter 4: Happy People Don't Sweat the Small Stuff 14

Chapter 5: 6 Reasons Your Emotions Are Getting In The Way Of Your Success 17

Chapter 6: *Don't Live Your Life In Regret* 22

Chapter 7: There's No Time for Regrets 25

Chapter 8: *How to Hold Yourself Accountable For Everything That You Do* 28

Chapter 9: Dealing With Stress from All Angles 30

Chapter 10: Happy People Are Optimistic 33

Chapter 11: 8 Ways to Discover What's holding You Back From Achieving Your Visions 35

Chapter 12: *Improve Everything By 1%* 39

Chapter 13: Saying Yes To Things 42

Chapter 14: Other People's Problems Are Not Always Your Problems 47

Chapter 15: 10 Habits For Good Health 50

Chapter 16: Becoming High Achievers 53

Chapter 17: Choose Getting into Nature for Better Mood and Happiness 58

Chapter 18: Feeling like You're Drowning in Stuff 60

Chapter 19: How To Do A Life Audit To Get Your Life Together ... 62

Chapter 20: The Problem With Immediate Gratification 65

Chapter 21: *How to Build Skills That Are Valuable* 70

Chapter 22: 10 Habits Holding You Back - The Power Of Habits 73

Chapter 23: How To Rid Yourself of Distraction 78

Chapter 24: Get Motivated Even When You Don't Feel Like It 82

Chapter 25: How To Stop Being A Narcissist 85

Chapter 26: 10 Habits of Larry Ellison 88

Chapter 27: *Treat Failure Like A Scientist* 92

Chapter 28: Happy People Choose to Exercise 95

Chapter 29: 4 Ways to Deal with Feelings of Inferiority When Comparing to Others 97

Chapter 30: How To Deal With Uncertainty? 99

Chapter 31: *Happy People Give Freely* 103

Chapter 32: How To Develop An Incredible Work Ethic 105

Chapter 33: *Resist Temptations For Success* 108

Chapter 34: The Magic of Journaling 111

Chapter 35: How To Let Your Values Drive Your Choices 114

Chapter 36: How Smart Do You Have To Be To Succeed 117

Chapter 1:
What Is The Meaning of Life?

The question of the meaning of life is perhaps one that we would rather not ask, for <u>fear</u> of the answer or lack thereof. Still today, many people believe that we, humankind, are the creation of a supernatural entity called God, that God had an intelligent purpose in creating us, and that this intelligent purpose is "the meaning of life".

I do not propose to rehearse the well-worn arguments for and against the existence of God, and still less to take a side. But even if God exists, and even if He had an intelligent purpose in creating us, no one really knows what this purpose might be, or that it is especially meaningful. The Second Law of Thermodynamics states that the entropy of a closed system—including the universe itself—increases up to the point at which equilibrium is reached, and God's purpose in creating us, and, indeed, all of nature, might have been no more lofty than to catalyse this process much as soil organisms catalyse the decomposition of organic matter.

If our God-given purpose is to act as super-efficient heat dissipaters, then having no purpose at all is better than having this sort of purpose—because it frees us to be the authors of our purpose or purposes and so to lead truly dignified and meaningful lives. In fact, following this logic, having no purpose at all is better than having any kind of pre-determined purpose, even more traditional, uplifting ones such as serving God or improving our karma.

In short, even if God exists, and even if He had an intelligent purpose in creating us (and why should He have had?), we do not know what this purpose might be, and, whatever it might be, we would rather be able to do without it, or at least to ignore or discount it. For unless we can be free to become the authors of our own purpose or purposes, our lives may have, at worst, no purpose at all, and, at best, only some unfathomable and potentially trivial purpose that is not of our own choosing.

You might yet object that talk about the meaning of life is neither here nor there because life is merely a prelude to some form of eternal afterlife, and this, if you will, is its purpose.

But I can marshal up at least four arguments against this position:

- It is not at all clear that there is, or even can be, some form of eternal afterlife that entails the survival of the personal ego.

- Even if there were such an afterlife, living for ever is not in itself a purpose. The concept of the afterlife merely displaces the problem to one remove, begging the question: what then is the purpose of the afterlife? If the afterlife has a pre-determined purpose, again, we do not know what that is, and, whatever it is, we would rather be able to do without it.

- Reliance on an eternal afterlife not only postpones the question of life's purpose, but also dissuades or at least discourages us from determining a purpose or purposes for what may be the only life that we do have.

Chapter 2:
The Chosen Ones Choose Themselves

Many people will judge, maybe even curse if I were to say that 'Success is not for everyone!'. You heard me! Not everyone deserves success. It is not something I'd say to demotivate someone. The reality is that most people don't have a lot of success stories to tell.

The wealthy are mostly the people to get a chance to talk about the mountains of success that they had and are still having. Now, I know what you might say. You might say that you need to be rich to have opportunities, and you need a lot of opportunities to be successful at maybe a few.

You might say that not all people have the luxury to have a choice when it comes to their chances in life. And I know it is true for 99 percent of the people. But you don't understand the philosophy of success.

Success is not an incident! Success is not sheer luck! Success is a temptation, a feeling, a dream, an emotion, a lifestyle! It is something that you choose to do and only you can stay on the path because you were the only one to see the dust particles in a single ray of sun in a dark room.

You cannot expect to be unique if you follow everyone else like sheep. You will always end up in a herd of stupid nonproductive people if you keep following blindly and not following your own instincts. How do you expect to discover who you truly are?

Let me give you a hint. Do you want to know your true colors? Go on in your room. Shut the door, switch the lights lay down with heads up, and think of all the things you did just because you saw someone else doing it. Think of the goals you choose because you saw how appealing it looks on a social media post. Now try to think of a single thing that you did just because it struck you one day out of the blue and you had this magical feeling of pursuit.

The people who have everything in the world are the people who the world treats as kings. These people had a time when had no one and they didn't want anyone. Because what they wanted to do was so far-fetched that only they could comprehend the outcomes that no one had ever thought of before.

Life has a process for everyone. Life chooses everyone. It might not be now, but it will someday. But when you are the chosen one, always stay ahead of everyone else. Don't try to be selfless, because it is always the survival of the fittest. It always has and it always will be.

You try to slow down for someone else, and they will climb up while dragging you down. If you think you will get some recognition and this will give you the confidence to do more, then you had it all wrong from the start.

Chapter 3:
How To Accept Yourself No Matter What

There are many reasons why it may be difficult to accept yourself. Just hearing one that resonates for you can bring relief because you realize you are not alone — someone else has been there, someone else understands. Here are some of the reasons self-acceptance can be hard and the antidotes you can practice to gradually accept yourself more and more— step one and two from the change steps listed above.

See which ones resonate for you.

1. You Think You're At Fault

You may blame yourself for something that happened in your life, especially events that may have occurred in your early years. For example, you may believe you're the cause of conflict in your parents' relationship or even their divorce.

Antidote: give the responsibility back. It was never yours to own.

2. You Think You're Not Worthy.

You began to feel inadequate as a child and carried that belief into your adult life.

Antidote: you are worthy simply because you exist. In between your confusion, self-doubt, and angst, there is so much goodness in you.

Instead of focusing on your failings, start to believe in and accentuate your positives. Take time to learn to love yourself

3. You Didn't Have Positive Roles Models.

If one of your parents or primary caregivers didn't accept themselves, you may be modeling their behavior.

Antidote: find positive roles models now, people who love, accept and care for themselves with confidence. Follow their lead.

4. You've Made Self-Acceptance Conditional.

You believe you need to achieve something before you can fully accept yourself. You're waiting to complete your education, earn a specific amount of money, or get a promotion at your job.

But even when you make it to a goal post, you find you still can't accept yourself. You tell yourself you need to reach the next before you do.

Antidote: take the conditions off and accept your whole self right, now.

5. You Are Trying To Live Up To Societal Norms.

There's so much pressure to live up to societal norms within most families, at school, and in the advertisements that abound all around you.

You may not accept who you are because you think you should be someone else—the grade a student or the perfect mom and wife with the ideal figure and a corporate job too.

Antidote: break the societal norms! Make new ones! Make your own! Decide who you want to be for yourself.

6. Your Circle Is Not Supportive.

It's difficult to feel good about yourself if your partner, friends, or employer are constantly putting you down. I know this for myself. I had a harsh boss for many years. His constant criticism eroded my self-confidence.

Antidote: surround yourself with people who love, appreciate, and support you, one person at a time. Leave unsupportive situations.

7. You've Been Traumatized.

The experience of shock or early childhood trauma can trigger shame or the mistaken belief that you were somehow responsible.

Antidote: know this is a common reaction in trauma, but it doesn't make it true. Find a trauma therapist who can help you heal the trauma and transform these incorrect beliefs.

You can't go from zero self-acceptance to accepting yourself just like that. But it doesn't have to take eons either.

Positive repetition works over time. It actually modifies your brain. Use these four steps to change your response:

1. "first, label the response you want to change."

2. "second, identify the new response that you want to develop."

3. "third, explore what factors might reduce the unwanted response and boost the desired response."

4. "lastly, repeatedly practice the new response so that it becomes ingrained."

Start on the path of self-acceptance now. You'll feel very different in a few months and surely in a few years to come. You'll grow in self-love, self-acceptance, and your ability to care for yourself.

Won't that be so much better than rejecting yourself?

Chapter 4:
Happy People Don't Sweat the Small Stuff.

Stress follows a peculiar principle: when life hits us with big crises—the death of a loved one or a job loss—we somehow find the inner strength to endure these upheavals in due course. It's the little things that drive us insane day after day—traffic congestion, awful service at a restaurant, an overbearing coworker taking credit for your work, meddling in-laws, for example.

It's all too easy to get caught up in the many irritations of life. We overdramatize and overreact to life's myriad tribulations. Under the direct influence of anguish, our minds are bewildered, and we feel disoriented. This creates stress, which makes the problems more difficult to deal with.

The central thesis of psychotherapist Richard Carlson's bestselling ***Doesn't Sweat The Small Stuff… And It's All Small Stuff*** (1997) is this: to deal with angst or anger, we need not some upbeat self-help prescriptions for changing ourselves, but simply a measure of perspective.

Perspective helps us understand that there's an art to understand what we should let go of and what we should concern ourselves with. It is important to focus our efforts on the important stuff and not waste time on insignificant and incidental things.

I've previously written about my favorite 5-5-5 technique for gaining perspective and guarding myself against anger erupting: I remove myself from the offending environment and contemplate if whatever I'm getting worked up over is of importance. I ask myself, "Will this matter in 5 days? Will this matter in 5 months? Will this matter in 5 years?"

Carlson stresses that there's always a vantage point from which even the biggest stressor can be effectively dealt with. The challenge is to keep making that shift in perspective. When we achieve that "wise-person-in-me" perspective, our problems seem more controllable and our lives more peaceful.

Carlson's prescriptions aren't uncommon—we can learn to be more patient, compassionate, generous, grateful, and kind, all of which will improve the way we feel about ourselves and how other people feel when they are around us.

Some of Carlson's 100 recommendations are trite and banal—for example, "make peace with imperfection," "think of your problems as potential teachers," "remember that when you die, your 'in-basket' won't be empty," and "do one thing at a time." Others are more informative:

- Let others have the glory
- Let others be "right" most of the time
- Become aware of your moods, and don't allow yourself to be fooled by the low ones
- Look beyond behavior
- Every day, tell at least one person something you like, admire, or appreciate about them.
- Argue for your limitations, and they're yours
- Resist the urge to criticize
- Read articles and books with entirely different points of view from your own and try to learn something.

Chapter 5:
6 Reasons Your Emotions Are Getting In The Way Of Your Success

Do you ever ponder on why your new year's resolutions fail miserably? It is primarily because of the toxic emotions and our negative thoughts of the past that keeps us stuck with the same patterns and regrets. We can try to change and manage our attitudes well, but the emotions are out of our hands. So even though we can't control what we feel, we must confront them to achieve our goals and resolutions.

A therapist in Tarzana, California, Vicki Botnick, explains that any emotion – even elation, joy, or others you would typically view as positive – can intensify to a point where it becomes difficult to control.

Here are 6 Reasons why emotions are getting in the way of your success

1. **You let your emotions rule you**

Most of us are clueless about taking control of our emotions and how they affect our productivity. But we must manage them if we strive to achieve our goals. Emotions are an instant response to a specific trigger. All of our emotions are interlinked with each other. For example, we can't taste the satisfaction of joy if we don't go through any pain, or we can't enjoy courage without being fearful first. All of these emotions are what make us human. Embracing both negative and positive emotions are essential, but if they start to get in the way of your success, then you must take action and act upon them.

2. Anger.

"The greatest remedy for anger is a delay." - Thomas Paine.

Anger is the majorly common emotion that humankind feels. This negative emotion can result from frustrations, conflicts, mistreatment, or interpersonal conflicts, or is sometimes triggered by an event or experience that happened in the past. For example, suppose you studied really hard for a test but didn't get the expected grade. The next time when you're willing to give it another try, you won't study as much as you did the first time because you'll remember your previous failed attempt. You will re-live your failure and will eventually become frustrated and demotivated. The best thing to do in this scenario is just to take some time off and breathe. Distance yourself from everything and get yourself to calm down before making any decision. Ask yourself then, are you too hard on yourself? Are you trying to do everything at once that's causing you to get upset? Have you set the bar too high? Ponder on these questions and then look for the solutions calmly. Being angry about the things you can't control is pointless, as anger feeds more anger, and you would get stuck in an endless loop of resentment and frustration. Seek solutions on the things you can control and be patient.

3. Fear.

The fear of failure is perhaps the worst emotion we can endure. It snatches away even the slightest chance of taking that first step to achieving our dreams and goals. The reasons why we are so afraid of failures may vary from person to person. Some people can't digest that they are full of flaws and that failure is the most crucial step towards leading a successful life. They want to win no matter what. Others might feel that they are not good enough if they can't achieve something. Most people don't admit that they have fears. Fear can either be your greatest friend or your worst enemy; it all depends on how you treat it, whether you look into its eyes and face it or run from it. Living fearlessly doesn't mean that a person isn't afraid of anything, but rather that the person has befriended his fears and is now dancing with them. One shouldn't run away from the challenges that the world throws at him, but stand up to them bravely and face them. Make a list of all the things that scare you or are distracting you from achieving your goals. And then work towards them until they no longer bother you or gets in the way of your success. A famous African proverb states, "Smooth seas do not make skillful sailors."

4. **Envy.**

Bertrand Russell once said, "Beggars do not envy millionaires, though of course, they will envy other beggars who are more successful." Envy and jealousy are the two strongest emotions that mankind has experienced. Although they go hand in hand with each other, there is still a slight difference between them. Being envious wants the other person's things, while jealousy wants the other person's recognition from others. Whenever things tend to go south, we start to become envious of those who are successful. We compare ourselves to them, idealize their successes, and in the process, we lose ourselves. We shift our focus from our signs of progress to being demotivated and stressed out. Pain is an indicator of progress. When we stretch our minds beyond our comfort zone, we feel pain. This pain is the indication that we should move forward and not run away. We shouldn't compare our initial progress to those who have been striving for years. Everyone has their own pace. We should focus on ourselves and setting our potentials free.

5. **Guilt.**

The guilt of doing something else or saying something else instead of what you already did or said will forever haunt us. Guilt gets us stuck in the past rather than live in the present moment. There is a term in psychology, The Zeigarnik Effect, which refers that people remember uncompleted tasks more than the completed ones. They then blame themselves for not doing it sooner or better. Our mindset is often linked with productivity blame, where we feel bad for achieving something or not working hard enough. We tend to punish ourselves emotionally and get the idea that we can never reach our goals. But it is essential to take some time off and treat yourself with kindness and empathy. Don't over-pressurize yourself. Self-appreciate and become a better version of yourself in the process. "Mistakes are always forgivable if one dares to admit them." - Bruce Lee.

6. **Sadness.**

"We must understand that sadness is an ocean, and sometimes we drown, while other days, we are forced to swim." - R.M. Drake.

Feeling sad or low on energy crushes productivity and enthusiasm. We feel demotivated and can't focus on our tasks. Sadness makes us feel secluded and isolated. We must embrace this emotion at our own pace, but we shouldn't hide away from whatever it is that's bothering us. Start again slowly with your productivity, make slight progress, start rechallenging yourself. But don't do all of this unless you feel okay again.

Conclusion:

Understanding how your emotions are getting in the way of your productivity requires practice. Self-awareness is the key to know yourself better, so you can deal with your emotions efficiently. Please pay close attention to what your feelings are trying to tell you rather than running away from them.

Chapter 6:
Don't Live Your Life In Regret

Take this for a lesson today; There is no greater pain than that of regret.

Hopelessness is one thing that can crack a soul, but nothing is more hurting than that of lifelong regret. We take up things in our life that we deem helpful for the times to come. But never do we ever take risks, just because we want to have a smooth uncomplicated life.

Life was never meant to be lived as reading off a paper. Neither can you expect it to be a smooth walk on a beach? There are always some pebbles on the way and always some hedges where you need to twist and turn to fit and climb.

We all will eventually o through a period of endless questioning where we judge our every step and every decision whether if it was bad or not good enough!

But why are we indulging in this waste of time when we have so much better things to do right now in this present time slot.

When you are on a long journey, nothing will make sense. When you are on your path to greatness, you will always look back and get drawn back a little every time.

But once you reach the top, you will have a final look back into your past and everything will make sense in a split second.

Life is a roller coaster and we all have baggage. We must have because no one can have lived a long life and have a straight, plain, and colorless script where nothing happened out of the ordinary.

The uncertainty of life is what defines life to its true reality.

We, humans, are a combination of deterministic and non-deterministic behavior where we get triggered on thoughts of shame and failure but rarely do we learn to listen to those failures and try to change our habits.

Things have a course of happening and we always get behind the things that take most of us down the lane. That is where we feel the walk of shame and remember the feeling for the rest of our life.

But why do we feel the urge to remain connected to our shameful past? What needs do we have with feeling shame? Why do we need to remember and regret the things that the world has forgotten a long time ago? Why do we need to keep those memories alive?

A billion incidents are happening every second and we try to keep all our baggage with us till the day we take it with us to our graves.

What we should be doing is to forgive everyone and especially ourselves, to release some positive energy and make some space for the happy times that are to come.

We should let those happy moments erase all our regrets and ease our path for the best future that time could ever earn us. But what you should do ultimately, is to regret what you haven't done yet, rather than what you have done!

Chapter 7:
There's No Time for Regrets

Regret. Guilt. Shame.

These are three of the darkest emotions any human will ever experience. We all feel these things at different points in our lives, especially after making a "bad" decision. There are certain situations some of us would rewind (or delete) if we could. The reality is, however, there is an infinite number of reasons we should never regret any of the decisions we make in our lives.

Here are 7 of them:

1. Every decision allows you to take credit for creating your own life.

Decisions are not always the result of thoughtful contemplation. Some of them are made on impulse alone. Regardless of the decision, when you made it, it was something you wanted, or you would not have done it (unless someone was pointing a gun at your head).

Be willing to own the decisions you make. Be accountable for them. Take responsibility and accept them.

2. By making any decision involving your heart, you have the chance to create more love in the world by spreading yours.

Your love is a gift.

Once you decide to love, do it without reservation. By fully giving of yourself, you expand your ability to express and receive love. You have added to the goodness of our universe by revealing your heart to it.

3. By experiencing the disappointment that might come with a decision's outcome, you can propel yourself to a new level of emotional evolution.

You aren't doing yourself any favors when you try to save yourself from disappointment. Disappointment provides you with an opportunity to redefine your experiences in life. By refining your reframing skills, you increase your resilience.

4. "Bad" decisions are your opportunity to master the art of self-forgiveness.

When you make a "bad" decision, *you* are the person who is usually the hardest on yourself. Before you can accept the consequences of your decision and move on, you must forgive yourself. You won't always make perfect choices in your life. Acknowledge the beauty in your human imperfection, then move forward and on.

5. Because of the occasional misstep, you enable yourself to live a Technicolor life.

Anger. Joy. Sadness. These emotions add pigment to your life. Without these things, you would feel soulless. Your life would be black and white.

Make your decisions with gusto. Breathe with fire. You are here to live in color.

6. Your ability to make a decision is an opportunity to exercise the freedom that is your birthright.

How would you feel if you had no say in those decisions concerning your life? Would you feel powerless? Restricted? Suffocated?

Now, focus on what it feels like to make the decisions you want to make. What do you feel? Freedom? Liberty? Independence?

What feelings do you *want* to feel? Freedom. Liberty. Independence.

As luck would have it, the freedom you want is yours. Be thankful for it in every decision you make, "good" or "bad."

7. When you decide to result in ugly aftermath, you refine what you *do* want in your life.

It's often impossible to know what you want until you experience what you don't want. With every decision, you will experience consequences. Use those outcomes as a jumping-off point to something different (and better) in your future.

Chapter 8:

How to Hold Yourself Accountable For Everything That You Do

Staying on top of your work can be difficult without a manager over your shoulder. So how exactly do you manage yourself? I don't know about you, but I have a problem. I am ambitious; I am full of great ideas. I am also, however, extremely undisciplined. But the other day, I had an idea. What if I became "my manager"? Not a bad idea.

Contrary to what the multi-million dollar management training industry says, I don't think management is rocket science (though I am not saying it is easy). A good manager motivates and supports people and makes people accountable. To manage ourselves, we simply need to take concrete steps to motivate ourselves and make ourselves accountable.

1. **Create a Personal Mission Statement**

I think we get so caught up in the mundane details of daily life that we often lose track of why we're here, what we want, and, most importantly, what we value. Manage yourself by finding a way to integrate your values into what you do. Write your mission statement.

My mission statement, at the moment, is this: "To live simply and give selflessly, and to work diligently towards financial independence and the opportunities such independence will afford me."

Your mission statement doesn't have to be profound or poetic – it just needs to convey your core values and define why you do what you do each day. (Hint: If you can't find a mission statement that fits your current career or life, maybe it is time for a change!

2. **Set Micro-Goals**

There are countless benefits to writing down goals of all sizes. Annual, five-, and ten-year goals can help you expand on your mission statement because you know you are working towards a tangible result. But long-term goals are useless unless you have a strategy to achieve them. Manage yourself by setting micro-goals.

What is a micro-goal? I like to think of it as a single action that, when accomplished, serves as a building block to a much larger goal.

For example, the resolution to make a larger-than minimum monthly payment on a credit card balance is a micro goal. Each month you successfully increase your payment, you are closer to your big goal of getting out of debt.

At work, a micro-goal might involve setting up an important client meeting. Getting all the elements for a meeting in place is one step towards a larger goal of winning or increasing a particular business relationship.

A micro goal is not, however, anything that goes on your to-do list. Responding to a customer inquiry or cleaning out your cubicle is not a micro-goal unless, of course, you have bigger goals to specifically involving that customer or to get more organized.

Chapter 9:
Dealing With Stress from All Angles

Stress is something that every human being suffers at some point in their lives. Whether it is A bad day at school or an exam gone wrong, there is no limit to the reasons behind stress. But some people deal with stress which does not only have one reason. In today's day and age, the world has become so fast that people do not have time for themselves. In situations where one gets the feeling of being beaten or lost, one should never give up and should always focus on what is good.

As stated by Dr. Helen Odessky, "I would encourage [you to] try A stress relief activity three times before you give up on it. "She further explains that when A person is undergoing A state of stress, the body resists any relaxation exercise or practice, so trying it out A few times increases the chances of that practice to work. Sometimes, A person's routine can make them stressed, for example, and if somebody wakes up just before the office starts, they would have to rush for the office and is likely to skip breakfast. If this is A trigger for the stress to kick in, stress can be overcome by simply changing the morning routine and giving the body enough time to function properly before the office starts.

The most important thing to notice in A stressful person is that they either breathe too quickly or too slowly because, in A time of stress, breathing is one aspect that often gets ignored. Breathing is the key for the body to function properly, so trying out A simple inhale/exhale exercise in A time of stress can help to overcome it quickly. Another thing one does in A time of stress is that they start to overthink, and the majority of the thought are negative ones. So, according to bizzie gold, who is A personal development and wellness expert, writing down your thoughts in A time of stress is A good way of letting them out. Especially the bad ones. This way, your brain would be at ease, and you can always reflect on these thoughts once the stressful period is over. Physical exercise is another good way to overcome stress as it produces endorphins, which instantly lighten the mood. The repetitive physical movements can help to fend off the bad thoughts and reset the mind, which leads to A stress-free state of mind. Even during A busy day, going for A short workout such as running can help ease the mind. Lastly, A very effective yet ignored way of overcoming stress is cleaning up the space around you. A dirty or messy space can also lead to bad thoughts, so opting for A quick tidy-up is A very good practice for overcoming stress.

Stress is indeed A very harmful feeling which can make the affected person do harmful things like drugs or alcohol, which can further lead to A messed up life. So overcoming stress before it gets A hold of you is always the better option. The exercises explained above may seem very simple but are very effective for people who deal with stress. Being grateful for what you already have is A great way to overcome stress. Find people who make you feel good in your time of need. We only have one life; why not enjoy it fully and not waste it stressing over meaningless stuff.

Chapter 10:
Happy People Are Optimistic

Beyond the simple reality that optimists are happier people (and happiness is what you're striving for), optimism has other benefits as well. So, if you want to achieve greater happiness, try being optimistic for a day.

Optimists enjoy a greater degree of academic success than pessimists do. Because optimistic students think it's possible for them to make a good grade, they study hardier and they study smarter. They manage the setting in which they study and they seek help from others when they need it. (Optimism, it turns out, is almost as predictive of how well students do in college as the SAT.)

Optimists are more self-confident than pessimists are. They believe in *themselves* more than fate.

Optimists are more likely to be problem-solvers than pessimists are. When pessimistic students get a D on a test, they tend to think things like: "I knew I shouldn't have taken this course. I'm no good at psychology." The optimistic student who gets a D says to herself, "I can do better. I just didn't study enough for this test. I'll do better next time." And she will.

Optimists welcome second chances after they fail more than pessimists do. Optimistic golfers always take a *mulligan* (a redo swing without penalty). Why? Because they expect to achieve a better result the second time around.

Optimists are more socially outgoing than pessimists are. Socially outgoing folks believe that the time they spend with other human beings makes them better in some way — smarter, more interesting, more attractive. Unfortunately, pessimists see little, if any, benefit from venturing out into the social world.

Optimists are not as lonely as pessimists are. Because pessimists don't see as much benefit from socializing with others, they have far fewer social and emotional connections in their lives, which is what loneliness is all about.

Optimists utilize social support more effectively than pessimists do. They aren't afraid to reach out in times of need.

Optimists are less likely to blame others for their misfortune than pessimists are. When you blame someone else for your troubles, what you're really saying is, "You're the *cause* of my problem and, therefore, you have to be the *solution* as well." Optimists have just as many troubles as pessimists throughout life — they just accept more responsibility for dealing with their misfortune.

Optimists cope with stress better than pessimists do. Pessimists worry, optimists act. A patient with coronary heart disease who is pessimistic "hopes and prays" that he doesn't have another heart attack anytime soon. The optimistic heart patient leaves little to chance — instead, he exercises regularly, practices his meditation exercises, adheres to a low-cholesterol diet, and makes sure he always gets a good night's sleep.

Chapter 11:
8 Ways to Discover What's holding You Back From Achieving Your Visions

We all have dreams, and I have no questions; you have made attempts at seeking after your goals. Oh, as a general rule, life's battles get the better of you and keep you down. The pressure of everyday life, again and again, puts you down. Regardless of your determination, devotion, and want, alone, they are not enough.

Being here exhibits you are not able to settle for a mediocre life and hidden desires. To help you in your goal of seeking after your objectives, you must become acquainted with those things keeping you down. When you do, you will want to eliminate every single reason keeping you down.

1. Fear
The deep-rooted foe is very likely a critical factor in keeping many of you from seeking after your objectives. It prevents you from acting, making you scared of venturing out. Dread is the thing that keeps you down. Dread is one reason why we don't follow what we truly need throughout everyday life.
- Fear of disappointment
- Fear of dismissal
- Fear of mocking

- Fear of disappointment

Quit allowing your feelings of fear to keep you down!

2. Procrastination

Putting things off till the following week, one month from now, one year from now, and regularly forever. You're not exactly sure the thing you're hanging tight for, but rather when whatever it happens, you'll be prepared to start seeking after your objectives. Be that as it may, this day never comes. Your fantasy stays as just a fantasy. Putting things off can just keep you down.

Quit allowing your Procrastination to keep you down!

3. Justifications

Do you find yourself procrastinating and making excuses for why you can't start working toward your goals? Those that succeed in accomplishing their objectives can overcome obstacles. So many individuals make excuses for themselves, believing they can't achieve a better career, start their own business, or find their ideal lifemate.

- It isn't the correct time
- I am insufficient
- I am too old/young

Don't allow your excuses to hold you back any longer!

4. Lack of Confidence

Lack of confidence in yourself or your ability to achieve your goals will inevitably hold you back. Our actions, or lack thereof, are influenced by what goes on in our subconscious mind. We have self-limiting and negative beliefs that may be preventing us from enjoying an extraordinary life.

Nothing will be able to stop you if you believe in yourself. Bringing your limiting beliefs into focus will help you achieve your objectives.

Don't let your lack of confidence keep you back!

5. There Isn't A Big Picture

Others refer to what I call a breakthrough goal as a BHAG - Big Hairy Audacious Goal. A goal is what you need to keep you motivated and drive you to achieve it every day. Start small and dream big. You'll need a strong enough passion to propel you forward. Your ambitions will not motivate you until you first dream big.

For your objectives to be beneficial to you, they must assist you in realizing your ambitions. Those lofty ambitions. Goals can only motivate you, help you stay focused, and help you make the adjustments you need to make, as well as provide you the fortitude to overcome difficulties as you chase your big-picture dreams if they matter to you.

Stop allowing your big picture to stifle your progress!

6. Inability To Concentrate

Your chances of success are slashed every moment you lose focus. When we spread our focus too thin, we dilute our effort and lose the ability to focus on the most significant tasks. When you're pulled in a lot of different directions and have a lot of conflicting priorities fighting for your attention, it's easy to lose track of what's important. Any attempts to achieve vital goals will be harmed as a result of this.

Stop allowing your lack of concentration to keep you back!

7. Failure to Make a Plan

Finally, if you don't have a strategy, it's easy to become lost along the route. Consider driving across the country without a map, say from London to Glasgow. While you have a rough route in mind, there are many lands to cover and a lot of false turns and dead ends to be avoided. You can get there with the help of a GPS. It plots your path and creates a plan for you. A plan provides you with the road map you need to reach your objectives. This is the process of determining what you need to accomplish to reach your objectives. This is where you put in the time and effort to write out a plan of the steps you need to follow, the resources you'll need, and the amount of time you'll need to invest.

Stop allowing the lack of a strategy holds you back!

8. Not Keeping Track of Your Progress and Making Necessary Modifications

Goals, by their very nature, take time to attain. Therefore it's critical to keep track of your progress. You won't know what's working and what's not if you don't get quick and actionable feedback. You won't be able to tell when to alter or when to keep doing what you're doing. Anyone who is continuously successful in accomplishing their goals also reviews their goals and progress regularly. Regularly reviewing your goals allows you to make early modifications to stay on track.

Stop allowing not reviewing and adjusting your progress to hold you back!

Chapter 12:
Improve Everything By 1%

There is a concept in the athletic world known as the "Aggregation of Marginal Gains." It was first presented by Dave Brailsford, a performance coach for the British Cycling team.

He used to explain it as the "The 1% percent margin for improvement is always present for anything we do." What this means is that if you improve everything associated with your game by just 1 percent, these small changes will add up to show up as remarkable and rapid improvements.

We live a life of constant pushing and pulling, where we don't know what is going on and why is it happening but we still keep up with it because it is a job and not an option. But the truth is that we are not going anywhere anytime soon because we have not aced the art of living by perfection yet.

We cannot be perfect no matter what we try or what we get, but we can improve and it might get us better than most.

So how does this rule work? It is simple!

You take one aspect of your life and you work towards making a single thing better at a time. Let's say you were to start a business and have had your fair share of failures for all these years. So what to do now for a changed outcome?

You could start off by choosing a better thing to sell. You can look for better producers for better buying prices. The next thing you can do is to find better means of selling over the traditional mediums. And if you are e done that already, you can look for better markets to sell.

The right approach for a process lies in the small details that lead you to the final model.

There is always room for improvement in every aspect of life and this is the philosophy that we all lack. We expect things to get better once and for all in a single instant. But improvement is a time taking process and a constantly changing process.

We have convinced ourselves that change is only a meaningful thing once we have a large and prominent outcome that comes along. We expect to get bigger and better gains over an unrealistic amount of time with absolutely none to minimal effort.

I am not saying that you need to leave everything else and devote all your energies and time to a single target. But you need to improve little by little with small changes that are prominent on their own level. The results will improve but that will take some time and all you can do is hope for the best.

Improvement by 1% isn't noticeable for even the most alert people, but not trying it is the biggest blunder anyone can do. Your success is like your life cycle. You wait for getting taller, you wait for growing adult features and you wait for getting your first paycheck. Why do you expect to see results in one go?

Chapter 13:
Saying Yes To Things

Today we're going to talk about why saying yes can be a great thing for you and why you should do so especially in social invites.

Life you see is a funny thing. As humans, we tend to see things one dimensionally. And we tend to think that we have a long life ahead of us. We tend to take things for granted. We think we will have time to really have fun and relax after we have retired and so we should spend all our efforts and energy into building a career right now, prioritising it above all else. When faced with a choice between work and play, sometimes many of us, including myself choose work over social invites.

There were periods in my life that i routinely chose work over events that it became such a habit to say no. Especially as an entrepreneur, the interaction between colleagues or being in social events is almost reduced to zero. It became very easy and comfortable to live in this bubble where my one and only priority in life is to work work work. 24 hours, 7 days a week. Of course, in reality a lot of time was wasted on social media and Netflix, but u know, at least i could sort of pretend that i was kind of working all day. And I was sort of being productive and sort of working towards my goals rather than "wasting time on social events". That was what I told myself anyway.

But life does not work that way. As I prioritised work over all else, soon all the social invite offers started drying up. My constant "nos" were becoming evident to my social circle and I was being listed as perpetually unavailable or uninterested in vesting time or energy into any friendships or relationships. And as i retreated deeper and deeper into this black hole of "working remotely" i found myself completely isolated from new experiences and meeting new people, or even completely stopped being involved in any of my friend's lives.
I've successfully written myself out of life and I found myself all alone in it.

Instead of investing time into any meaningful relationships, I found that my closest friends were my laptop, tablet, phone, and television. Technology became my primary way of interacting with the world. And I felt connected, yet empty. I was always plugged in to wifi, but i lived my life through a screen instead of my own two eyes. My work and bedroom became a shell of a home that I spent almost all my time, and life just became sort of pointless. And I just felt very alone.

As I started to feel more and more like something was missing, I couldn't quite make out what it was that led me to this feeling. I simply though to myself, hey I'm prioritising work and my career, making money is what the internet tells me I should do, and not having a life is simply part of the price you have to pay... so why am I so incredibly unhappy?

As it turns out, as I hope many of you have already figured out at this point, that life isn't really just about becoming successful financially.

While buying a house, getting a car, and all that good stuff is definitely something that we should strive towards, we should not do so at the expense of our friends. That instead of saying no to them, we should start saying yes, at least once in a while. We need to signal to our friends that hey, yes even though I'm very busy, but I will make an effort to carve out time for you, so that you know I still value you in my life and that you are still a priority.

We need to show our friends that while Monday may not work for us, that I have an opening maybe 2 weeks later if you're still down. That we are still available to grow this friendship.

I came to a point in my life where I knew something had to change. As I started examining my life and the decisions I had made along the way with regards to my career, I knew that what I did wrong was saying no WAAAAAY too often. As I tried to recall when was the last time I actually when I went out with someone other than my one and only BFF, I simply could not. Of the years that went by, I had either said that I was too busy, or even on the off chances that I actually agreed to some sort of meetup, I had the habit of bailing last minute on lunch and dinner appointments with friends. And I never realized that i had such a terrible reputation of being a flaker until I started doing some serious accounting of my life. I had become someone that I absolutely detested without even realising it. I have had people bail on me at the very last minute before, and I hated that feeling. And whenever someone did that to me, I generally found it difficult to ask them out again because I felt that they weren't really that interested in meeting me anyway. That they didn't even bother to reschedule the appointment. And little did I know, I was becoming that very same person and doing the very thing that I hate to my friends. It is no wonder that I started dropping friends like flies with my terrible actions.

As I came to this revelation, I started panicking. It was as if a truck had hit me so hard that I felt that I was in a terrible accident. That how did I let myself get banged up to that extent?

I started scrolling through my contact lists, trying to find friends that might still want to hang out with me. I realized that my WhatsApp was basically dry as a desert, and my calendar was just work for the last 3 years straight with no meaningful highlights, no social events worth noting.

It was at this point that I knew I had made a huge mistake and I needed to change course immediately. Salvaging friendships and prioritising social activities went to the top of my list.

I started creating a list of friends that I had remotely any connection to in the last 5 years and I started asking them out one by one. Some of my friends who i had asked out may not know this, but at that point in my life, i felt pretty desperate and alone and I hung on to every meeting as if my life depended on it. Whilst I did manage to make some appointments and met up with some of them. I soon realized that the damage had been done. That my friends had clearly moved on without me... they had formed their own friends at work and elsewhere, and I was not at all that important to have anymore. It was too little too late at that point and there was not much I could do about it. While I made multiple attempts to ask people out, I did not receive the same offers from people. It felt clearly like a one-way street and I felt that those people that I used to call friends, didn't really see me as one. You see growing a friendship takes time, sometimes years of consistent meetups before this person becomes indispensable in your life. Sharing unique experiences that allow your friends to see that you are truly vested in them and that you care about them and want to spend time with them. I simply did not give myself that chance to be integrated into someone's life in that same way, I did not invest that time to growing those friendships and I paid the price for it.

But I had to learn all these the hard way first before I can receive all the good that was about to come in the future.

Chapter 14:
Other People's Problems Are Not Always Your Problems

A friend was telling me about how she was visiting a very close friend of hers. This friend was going through a tough time, and when my friend left, she felt this heavy weight on her. She felt a responsibility to make sure her friend was okay. She also felt inadequate because she couldn't solve her friend's problems. I told her, "You can't be responsible for another person's happiness."

This can be really hard at times, especially if you're a nurturing person or just deeply love the person who's struggling. You want to be the fixer. You want to help them find the solution, make smart choices and see the light.

It might even feel selfish NOT to intervene and take care of things. After all, aren't friends and loved ones supposed to support each other?

Yes, of course.

But there's a difference between loving and supporting someone and trying to fix their problems and make them happy. One you can do. The other you simply cannot. Everyone is responsible for their own happiness. And, in fact, trying to take on the responsibility of another person's happiness can hurt them in the long run and deprive them of miracles. When you feel the urge to be the fixer, follow the three steps I outline below. You'll feel immediate relief. You can release the need to be responsible for another person's happiness. The weight will be lifted and you'll be able to show up for your loved one AND yourself.

1. Everyone has their own guidance system, whatever it is they believe in — whether that's intuition, angels, spirit guides, the Universe or God. Even if they don't believe, there is a guidance that *we* believe in that we have to trust is protecting them and guiding them. Have faith in other people's guidance systems.

2. I learned this a long time ago. You don't want to deprive somebody of their bottom. Every one of us has experienced turning points in our lives. These are opportunities to pivot, to hit our knees and fully surrender. When you try to fix someone else, you just get in the way of their potential to experience this miracle. I want to encourage you to really own that you are not here to deprive anyone of their bottom. Give them the chance to experience exactly what they need to experience, and don't be afraid of it.

3. We have to be conscious of the fact that it's not our responsibility to change, or heal, or help, or resurrect anyone from their own issues and feelings. We have to trust that no one will change until they want to be changed. When they're ready for that change to come into their life, then you'll be there. You'll be able to show up for them when they're ready to show up for themselves.

The most loving thing we can do for someone is accept them for who they truly are. By consistently practicing to accept someone where they are and see them with compassion, you realign with your true love nature. Through acceptance you release the resistance you've placed within your relationship, clearing the way for healing and for you to access more loving thoughts and feelings. When you change your thoughts and feelings about another person, you change your energy toward them. The other person will receive your shift in energy and feel released by you. Best of all, your shift in energy gives you momentum to continue releasing judgment so you can feel complete and free. Acceptance offers you this freedom.

Chapter 15:

10 Habits For Good Health

Good health is great wealth that we can be proud of. It cannot be equated with any amount of possessions. We follow the doctors' instructions to the latter when we fall sick because we want to regain back our good health. Here are ten habits for good health:

1. **Eating A Balanced Diet**

A balanced diet is one of the basic principles of proper nutrition. It is a simple yet essential pillar in building good health. A balanced meal should contain all the required nutrients – carbohydrates, proteins, vitamins, and water –in correct proportions.

Taking a balanced diet requires discipline. Regardless of how much you love one type of food, you cannot eat it alone at the expense of other meals. Diversified meals with different nutritional values are important to the body.

2. **Eating Fresh Food Only.**

Fresh food is that which is not stale. It is important to take fresh food because they are not contaminated with bacteria that accumulate over time due to poor storage. Stale food introduces bacteria to our bodies that will make us fall sick.

Poorly preserved food poses a risk to our health. Hotels and restaurants adhere to guidelines of proper food handling to prevent food poisoning to their customers. Taking fresh food reduces the risk of falling sick.

3. **Drinking Plenty Of Water.**

The body majorly consists of water. It is an important part of a balanced diet. Water helps us hydrate and stay fit. So important is water that our bodies require it more than it does food.

It is recommended to take eight glasses of water in a day for us to stay hydrated because it is excreted in large quantities and we need to replenish it. Taking plenty of water also helps improve our skin tone.

4. Doing Physical Exercise.

Physical exercise is very important but often overlooked. Our bodies need exercise to stay fit and keep off lifestyle diseases. Exercises are also a form of therapy.

We sweat when we do intense workouts and excrete toxic substances from the body that would have otherwise been left inside the body. Sweating as a result of exercise is extremely healthy for our bodies.

5. Avoiding Stress.

Stress causes poor mental health. It is caused by the pressure to attain a certain threshold beyond our ability. We strain our minds and bodies when we push ourselves to the wall and we may eventually fall sick.

Poor mental health will catch up with our general health and if not taken care of early, it can irreversibly affect us.

6. Regular Health Check-Ups.

We should not go to the hospital only when we fall sick because it could be too late to save an already worse situation. We should visit a dentist bi-annually and an optician annually.

We should check our blood sugar levels and body pressure often to monitor any slight changes and address them before it is late. Good health is arrived at when we take care of all the variables affecting us.

7. Observing Health And Hygiene Standards.

There are health guidelines that are in place although hardly adhered to. They seem trivial but are very important in sustaining good health. We should not despise them.

Some guidelines are washing hands before meals and after visiting the toilet. We are also required to change our toothbrushes after every three months to promote dental hygiene.

8. Avoiding Self-Prescription Of Medicine.

It is common practice to buy medicine over the counter without a doctor's advice or prescription. It could have been prescribed to our friends or relatives and we think that we could also use it.

Doing this is wrong because there are many variables a medical officer considers before prescribing medicine that could not apply to us. Instead of getting well, we could worsen our health.

9. Do Not Share Medicine.

To ensure good health, do not share your medication with anyone without seeking professional advice. Not only could it not work for you, but you will also be endangering their health because you will tamper with their dosage.

Sharing of medicine could make you take expired medicine if the first person stopped taking it a long time ago and you use it without checking on the expiry date.

10. Understanding The Importance Of Good Health.

You only value what is important. When you understand the importance of good health, you will value it and observe that you do not lose it.

Health education is key to good health. Reading health literature and attending health talks will inspire you to work towards good health.

In conclusion, health is wealth. Take care of it early enough before it is unmanageable and costly.

Chapter 16:
Becoming High Achievers

By becoming high achievers we become high off life, what better feeling is there than aiming for something you thought was unrealistic and then actually hitting that goal.

What better feeling is there than declaring we will do something against the perceived odds and then actually doing it.

To be a high achiever you must be a believer,

You must believe in yourself and believe that dream is possible for you.

It doesn't matter what anyone else thinks , as long as you believe,

To be a high achiever we must hunger to achieve.

To be an action taker.

Moving forward no matter what.

High achievers do not quit.

Keeping that vision in their minds eye until it becomes reality, no matter what.

Your biggest dream is protected by fear , loss and pain.

We must conquer all 3 of these impostors to walk through the door.

Not many do , most are still fighting fear and if they lose the battle, they quit.

Loss and pain are part of life.

Losses are hard on all of us.

Whether we lose possessions, whether we lose friends, whether we lose our jobs, or whether we lose family members.

Losing doesn't mean you have lost.

Losses are may be a tough pill to swallow, but they are essential because we cannot truly succeed until we fail.

We can't have the perfect relationship if we stay in a toxic one, and we can't have the life we desire until we make room by letting go of the old.

The 3 imposters that cause us so much terror are actually the first signs of our success.

So walk through fear in courage , look at loss as an eventual gain, and know that the pain is part of the game and without it you would be weak.

Becoming a high achiever requires a single minded focus on your goal, full commitment and an unnatural amount of persistence and work.

We must define what high achievement means to us individually, set the bar high and accept nothing less.

The achievement should not be money as money is not our currency but a tool.

The real currency is time and your result is the time you get to experience the world's places and products , so the result should always be that.

The holiday home , the fast car and the lifestyle of being healthy and wealthy, those are merely motivations to work towards. Like Carrots on a stick.

High achievement is individual to all of us, it means different things to each of us,

But if we are going to go for it we might as well go all out for the life we want, should we not?

I don't think we beat the odds of 1 in 400 trillion to be born, just to settle for mediocrity, did we?

Being a high achiever is in your DNA, if you can beat the odds, you can beat anything.

It is all about self-belief and confidence, we must have the confidence to take the action required and often the risk.

Risk is difficult for people and it's a difficult tight rope to walk. The line between risk and recklessness is razor thin.

Taking risks feels unnatural, not surprisingly as we all grew up in a health and safety bubble with all advice pointing towards safe and secure ways. But the reward is often in the risk and sometimes a leap of blind faith is required. This is what stops most of us - the fear of the unknown.

The truth is the path to success is foggy and we can only ever see one step ahead, we have to imagine the result and know it's somewhere down this foggy path and keep moving forward with our new life in mind.

Know that we can make it but be aware that along the path we will be met by fear, loss and pain and the bigger our goal the bigger these monsters will be.

The top achievers financially are fanatical about their work and often work 100+ hours per week.

Some often work day and night until a project is successful.

Being a high achiever requires giving more than what is expected, standing out for the high standard of your work because being known as number 1 in your field will pay you abundantly.

Being an innovator, thinking outside the box for better practices, creating superior products to your competition because quality is more rewarding than quantity.

Maximizing the quality of your products and services to give assurance to your customers that your company is the number 1 choice.

What can we do differently to bring a better result to the table and a better experience for our customers?

We must think about questions like that because change is inevitable and without thinking like that we get left behind, but if we keep asking that, we can successfully ride the wave of change straight to the beach of our desired results.

The route to your success is by making people happy because none of us can do anything alone, we must earn the money and to earn it we must make either our employers or employees and customers happy.

To engage in self-promotion and positive interaction with those around us, we must be polite and positive with everyone, even with our competition.

Because really the only competition is ourselves and that is all we should focus on.

Self-mastery, how can I do better than yesterday?

What can I do different today that will improve my circumstances for tomorrow.

Little changes add up to a big one.

The belief and persistence towards your desired results should be 100%, I will carry on until… is the right attitude.

We must declare to ourselves that we will do this , we don't yet know how but we know that we will.

Because high achievers like yourselves know that to make it you must endure and persist untill you win.

High achievers have an unnatural grit and thick skin , often doing what others won't, putting in the extra hours when others don't.

After you endure loss and conquer pain , the sky is the limit, and high achievers never settle until they are finished.

Chapter 17:
Choose Getting into Nature for Better Mood and Happiness

It's clear that hiking—and any physical activity—can reduce stress and anxiety. But, there's something about being in nature that may augment those impacts.

In [one recent experiment](#) conducted in Japan, participants were assigned to walk either in a forest or in an urban center (taking walks of equal length and difficulty) while having their heart rate variability, heart rate, and blood pressure measured. The participants also filled out questionnaires about their moods, stress levels, and other psychological measures.

Results showed that those who walked in forests had significantly lower heart rates and higher heart rate variability (indicating more relaxation and less stress) and reported better moods and less anxiety than those who walked in urban settings. The researchers concluded that there's something about being in nature that had a beneficial effect on stress reduction, above and beyond what exercise alone might have produced.

In [another study](#), researchers in Finland found that urban dwellers who strolled for as little as 20 minutes through an urban park or woodland reported significantly more stress relief than those who strolled in a city center.

The reasons for this effect are unclear, but scientists believe that we evolved to be more relaxed in natural spaces. In a now-classic laboratory experiment by Roger Ulrich of Texas A&M University and colleagues, participants who first viewed a stress-inducing movie, and were then exposed to color/sound videotapes depicting natural scenes, showed much quicker, more complete recovery from stress than those who'd been exposed to videos of urban settings.

These studies and others provide evidence that being in natural spaces—or even just looking out of a window onto a natural scene—somehow soothes us and relieves stress.

Gregory Bratman of Stanford University has found evidence that nature may impact our mood in other ways, too.

In one 2015 study, he and his colleagues randomly assigned 60 participants to a 50-minute walk in either a natural setting (oak woodlands) or an urban setting (along a four-lane road). Before and after the walk, the participants were assessed on their emotional state and on cognitive measures, such as how well they could perform tasks requiring short-term memory. Results showed that those who walked in nature experienced less anxiety, rumination (focused attention on negative aspects of oneself), and negative affect, as well as more positive emotions, in comparison to the urban walkers. They also improved their performance on the memory tasks.

Chapter 18:
Feeling like You're Drowning in Stuff

By drowning, the first thing that comes to mind is drowning in A pool of water. Well, drowning in life is almost the same as drowning in water. Every time you drown, you need the help of A lifeguard or any other guy who can drag you out and save you. The same is the case with drowning in life; if you don't dig deep enough to come out of this phase, you need the help of an expert to help you feel better. When A person feels like drowning in stuff, most of the time, the reason is the hectic daily routine or the rush of emotions. When emotions start to build up to an extent where they become A burden, the affected person feels like being drowned in these emotions. This can further lead to stress and anxiety. If the feeling is due to work, it's because the person is working more than his brain and body can handle. This mostly happens to students who are working part-time to manage their expenses. The burden of study is already A big one, and once coupled to the workload, it becomes A mountain of A burden where the student doesn't get any time to relax.

There are many ways to overcome this feeling. The most effective one is to let your emotions out. Some councilors are there to listen to one's problems and find the perfect solution to them. If A person chooses to remain silent, he will be overwhelmed by these emotions/thoughts, and that is when these feelings turn into depression and anxiety. When depression kicks in, it's even harder to get back on track than it is when you are starting to have feelings of drowning. Now for students who are also working, they should find A way to relax every now and then. Relaxation is always A good solution to these problems. Taking some time out for yourself can prove to be healthy for both the body and the brain. The mind always produces positive thoughts when it is relaxed. Overburdening can lead to negative emotions and thoughts, which can lead to the feeling of being drowned.

Working out can be very helpful in times like these. It releases A hormone called endorphin which actually helps with stress and gives you joyful emotions. When the body is engaged in repetitive motions, the brain gets distracted from all burdens and only focuses on the tasks at hand, which in this case is exercise. So focusing only on one task helps the brain to relax and heal from all of the thoughts that were being processed before. After the workout, the person feels very light and positive because of this short relaxation of the brain.

Mental health professionals are there for those who are having A hard time dealing with the feeling of being drowned in stuff. One should never feel ashamed of talking to somebody about matters like these because it is for their good. Relying on medicines and other relaxants can lead to improper functioning of the brain. Still, practicing habits like taking counsel from professionals or simply giving time to oneself can prove to be very healthy as it helps the mind to focus better. Giving up isn't the option; surviving and eventually living the best life is.

Chapter 19:
How To Do A Life Audit To Get Your Life Together

'New year, new me' - at least that's what most of us are thinking come January. It's the most common time of the year to want to make a change and sort your life out. But only 8% of us will keep to our New Year's resolutions, while the rest will struggle because we've either set too many, they are unrealistic - or we lose motivation entirely, get fed up, and drop all interest in it! So if you often find yourself asking, 'how can I change my life?' come to New Year, we suggest you try doing a Life Audit, which helps you take charge, assessing what you want and how to go and get it. It's a great way to learn how to improve your life for the better. Here's how...

1. START WITH POST-IT NOTES

Write everything down that you want to achieve, your goals, hopes, and dreams.

2. CATEGORIZE WHAT'S IMPORTANT

Group your Post-its into the areas that you want to work on. This could be health, finances, relationships, work, or exercise.

3. DO A NOW-OR-NEVER AUDIT

Once you've written down all your goals, stick them in a clear, visible place. Take a good look at each goal. Go through each one and ask yourself two questions, 'Is this important?' and 'Is this what I want?' If the answer is no and you think you'd be happy if you didn't do it, then get rid of it.

4. ASK SOME BIG QUESTIONS

Draw a circle, divide it into eight sections. Give each segment a part of your life, like relationships or fitness. This is where you ask yourself the important stuff! Which areas should you give more focus to, which bits need more work, and more importantly, which areas give your life meaning?

5. CLOSE THE GAP

Time to get practical! Choose realistic steps to bridge the gap between now and where you want to be. But remember - be realistic with yourself!

6. CREATE A TIMELINE

Decide what to do first and when you'd like to do it. You don't need to make big changes; many smaller steps can lead to a bigger and better change.

7. ENLIST SUPPORT

Friends and family are there for a reason. Let them know what you're doing, but choose carefully. You want someone who will support and won't question what you're doing and help you improve your life. The final step in a good life audit is summarizing your insights.

To do this, look for common themes and write out a clear picture of your life as it currently is. Having this life audit summary will help you decide what is adding value to your life, what you can let go of, and what actions you need to take.

Chapter 20: The Problem With Immediate Gratification

In today's topic we are going to talk about something that I am sure most of us struggle with every single day, myself included. I hope that by the end of this video, you will be able to make better decisions for yourself to maybe think further ahead rather than trying to get gratification right away.

There will be 5 areas that I want to talk about. Finance, social media, shopping, fitness, and career.

Alright if you're ready let's begin.

Let's start with the one thing that i think most of us will find it hard to resist. Shopping. For many of us, buying things can be a form of happiness. When we want something, our dopamine levels rise, and our attention is solely focused on acquiring that object whatever it may be. The anticipation of getting something is something very exciting and our bodies crave that sense of gratification in getting that product. Shopping can also be a form of distraction, maybe from work or from feeling stressed out. Shopping can also arise from boredom and the desire within us to satisfy our cravings for wanting things begins to consume us. This creates a real problem because after we attain the item, often we are not satisfied and start looking for the next thing. This creates a never ending cycle of seeking gratification immediately at the expense of our bank account. And we are soon left with a big hole in the wallet without realising it.

Before I talk about the solutions to this problem, i want to address the other 4 areas on the list.

The next one is social media. We tend to gravitate towards social media apps when we want to fill our time out of most probably boredom. At times when we are supposed to be working, instead of blocking out time to stay focused on the task at hand, we end up clicking on Instagram or Facebook, trying to see if there are any new updates to look at provided to us by the algorithm. Social media companies know this and they exploit our feeble nature with this cheap trick. Everytime we try to refresh a page, we seek immediate gratification. And we create within us a terrible habit hundreds of times a day, checking for updates that wastes hours away from our day.

The next area that maybe isn't so common is in the area of fitness. Instead of laying out a long term plan to improve our health and fitness through regular exercise and choosing healthy foods, we tend to want things happening for us immediately. We think and crave losing 10 pounds by tomorrow and set unrealistic targets that easily lets us down. Hence we seek for quick fix solutions that aim to cut short this process.

We may end up trying to take slimming pills, or looking for the next extreme fad or diet to get to our goals quicker. Many of them not ending the right way and can be potentially harmful for our health. For those that cannot control what they eat, in reverse they may seek immediate gratification by bingeing on a fast food meal, ice cream, chocolates, or whatever foods brings them the quickest source of comfort. Many a times at the expense of their weight. All these are also very harmful examples of immediate gratification.

The 4th area I want to talk about is something of bigger importance. And this may not resonate with everybody, but it is about having a career that also focuses on building a side stream of passive income rather than one that focuses on active income. You see active income is static. When we work, we get a pay check at the end of every month. We look forward to that paycheck and that becomes our gratification. But when we stop working, our income stream ceases as well. This desire to keep that paycheck every month keeps us in the jobs that we ate. And we only look towards our jobs as a means to an end, to get that gratification every month in X amounts of dollars. And for many of us who uses shopping as a way to fill the void left by our jobs, we end up using that Hard earned money to gratify ourselves even more, taking up loans and mortgages to buy more and more things. If this is you, you are definitely not alone.

The final area I want to address in the area of finance. And that goes hand in hand with spending money as well. You see for many of us, we fail to see the power that compounding and time has on our finances. When we spend money today instead of saving or investing it, we lose the potential returns that investments can do for our capital. While it may be fun for us to spend money now to acquire things, it may instead bring us 10x the joy knowing that this $1000 that we have invested could end up becoming $100000 in 30 years when it is time for us to retire. The effects of compounding are astonishing and I urge all of you to take a closer look at investing what you have now as you might be surprised at the amounts of returns you can get in 30-50 years or even sooner.

So where does this lead us in our fight against instant gratification? From the areas we have described, immediate gratification always seem to have a direct negative consequence. When we choose to satisfy our cravings for wanting things fast right now, we feed our inner desires that just keeps craving more. The point is that we will never be satisfied.

If however we take a long-term approach to things and make better decisions to delay our reward, many a times that feeling will return us more than 2 fold than if we had taken it immediately. The problem is that most of us do not possess this sort of patience. Our instinct tells us that now is the best time. But history and the law of life has repeatedly shown us that that is not always true. For many things in our life, things actually gets better with time. The more time you give yourself to heal from a heartbreak, the better it will get. The more time you invest your money, the greater the returns. The more time you spend time on doing something you love, the more happiness you will feel. The more time you put into eating moderately and exercising regularly, the faster you will see your body and health take shape. The more you resist turning on the social media app, the more you will find you won't need its attention after a while. The more time you spend with friends, the deeper the friendship.

The moral of the story in all of this is that giving yourself enough time is the key to success. Trying to get something quick and easy is not always the best solution to everything. You have to put in the time and energy required to see the fruits of your labour. And that is a law that we all have to realise and apply if we want to see true success. Rome isn't built in a day, so why would anything else be? We shouldn't rush through everything that we do expecting fast results and instant gratification.

So i challenge each and everyone of you to take a good look at the areas of your life that you expect fast results and things to happen immediately. See if any of the things that I have mentioned earlier resonates with you and see if you can modify the way you acquire things. I believe that with a little effort, we all can look towards a more rewarding path to success.

Chapter 21:
How to Build Skills That Are Valuable

The most valuable skills you can have in life and work are rarely taught in school, never show up on a resume, and are consistently overlooked and underappreciated. But there's some good news: It costs nothing to develop them, and you have the opportunity to do so.

Here's how

1. The Ability To Pay Attention

The shorter the average attention span gets, the more valuable your ability to focus becomes.

It's a huge competitive advantage to be able to pay attention to things for an extended period (and unfortunately, what passes for an extended period these days may be as little as 10 minutes).

The ability to pay attention helps you learn, communicate, be productive, and see opportunities others miss, among countless other things.

Two ways to improve your ability to pay attention:
- Practice single-tasking — read a book, watch a movie, or find some other thing to do for an extensive amount of time without allowing yourself to do anything else during that time. No side conversations. No checking your phone. Nothing but focus on that one thing.

- Become intentional with how you use your phone (and for the love of God, turn off your notifications!).

2. The Ability To Follow Directions

This one takes your improved ability to pay attention a step further.

Every aspect of your life and career involves directions —customers tell you what they want, your boss tells you what she needs to be done, and the people you care about tell you what they expect of you.

It's one thing to pay attention to instructions, but it's another to accurately follow them.

The best qualifications in the world won't land you a job if your application doesn't include the employer's requested details.

Your company won't care about your innovative ideas if they don't align with the problems they asked you to solve.

And the reason Facebook Ads may not work for you isn't that Facebook ads don't work — it's because you don't know the right ways to use them. The ability to follow directions serves as a filter that keeps otherwise qualified people from succeeding — and most of them don't even realize their struggles are rooted in this weakness.

Don't let that be you.

Two ways to improve your ability to follow directions:

1. Ask for directions on how to do things more often. Practice makes perfect.
2. Give directions to other people. Take something you know how to do (like write a blog post, for example), and write up directions to help others do it the way you do (like I did here). Teaching is a great

way to learn, and the process of creating directions will help you recognize the importance of little steps in directions you get from others.

The point of this post isn't to make you feel overwhelmed. The truth is, you already have these skills — we all do. But I wrote this because I've noticed many people don't think about these abilities as skills and therefore don't do much to hone them.

Chapter 22:
10 Habits Holding You Back - The Power Of Habits

Habits are powerful actions that have become part of our routine. They control our behavior and they determine our progress in life. Our success or failure is a culmination of our habits. Be careful what you adapt lest you regret it.

The habits we develop could either propel us to success or hold us back from achieving our dreams. Here is an insight into ten habits holding you back:

1. Idleness

Idling is not resting. It is staying aimlessly without doing anything. You cannot afford to idle around in the modern world where time is essential in doing business. Time waits for no one. It does not care whether or not you have an emergency, or whether or not you are disadvantaged in any way. The clock will continue ticking and you have to catch up with it.

Idling does not have to be illegal for you to shun it. Always find something to occupy your mind and you will comfortably keep evil thoughts at bay.

2. Assumptions

Assuming everything at face value has killed many dreams. Seek clarification on what is unclear. Life has no grey areas; it is all in black and white. Assumptions create conflicts because of different expectations from both parties.

Conflicts will hold you back because you will have to spend a lot of time resolving them instead of pursuing your dreams. They misplace your priorities in life.

3. Anger

It is an extremely strong emotion that can wreak havoc in your life to your disbelief. Anger is not entirely bad when properly managed. It is a powerful motivator of doing things that would otherwise appear impossible.

Some doors have been shut to your face because you were probably unable to control your anger. Manage your public display of emotions and you will overcome anger.

4. Misinformation

Wisdom is making decisions from a point of knowledge. Ignorance is responsible for a majority of the bad decisions that people make. When you successfully win the battle against ignorance, you will succeed where your predecessors failed.

Unless you eat the humble pie and revisit decisions made in ignorance, you will face the consequences of misinformed decisions. Acquaint yourself with what happens around you lest you regret it later. Knowledge is the weapon to fight ignorance.

5. Getting Stuck In The Past

The past has imprisoned many people and stagnated their progress in life. Everyone has made mistakes they are not proud of and would gladly write them off when given the opportunity. We may be condemned for our past mistakes but that does not define us.

Quit judging yourself on the scale of your past achievements. The present has different challenges to be handled differently and getting stuck in the past is a hindrance to your success.

6. Disconnect With The Future

What is holding you back could be your cluelessness about the future. It is the inevitable fate that everybody will face. Walking into it unarmed with skills on how to survive could hold you back from achieving your goals.

The earlier you connect your mind with the future and the trajectory you want your life to take, the better your chances at making it in life. Plan for the future lest you fail to realize your dreams.

7. Burning Bridges And Building Walls

Healthy relationships are the pillars upon which our lives are built upon. Do not carelessly sever ties with people because you could unknowingly block your destiny connectors.

Be slow to build walls with people or collapse bridges after you have used them because you never know when you will need to use them again. Do not allow unhealthy relationships to hold you back from realizing your dreams.

8. Toxicity

Poison can kill regardless of the quantity it is consumed. Toxicity can poison your dreams and kill the potential within you if it is not curbed on time. What could be holding you back is the baggage you carry around instead of renewing your mindset to face new challenges.

Make a purposeful change of heart to unchain yourself from the shackles of mental captivity. It could derail your progress or kill your dreams altogether.

9. Bad Company

The only cure to a bad company is shunning it and finding a new one that will bring out the best in you. The clique of friends you keep could push you towards your goals or hold you back from achieving your dreams.

You need fresh positive voices around you to preach hope and push you towards success. The power of a good company counters the negative one that holds you back.

10. Imitating Other People

The major hurdle to the youth is imitating other people's lifestyles. It makes you blind to the potential in you and you live a lie until the day you will live an authentic life.

Even though you have mentors you emulate, cut your cloth according to your size. A fake lifestyle will make you live an illusion that will prevent you from advancing in life.

In conclusion, these ten habits will hold you back from attaining the milestones you have set. Carefully work your way around them.

Chapter 23:
How To Rid Yourself of Distraction

Distraction and disaster sound rather similar.

It is a worldwide disorder that you are probably suffering from.

Distraction is robbing you of precious time during the day.

Distraction is robbing you of time that you should be working on your goals.

If you don't rid yourself of distraction, you are in big trouble.

It is a phenomenon that most employees are only productive 3 out of 8 hours at the office.

If you could half your distractions, you could double your productivity.

How far are you willing to go to combat distraction?

How badly do you want to achieve proper time management?

If you know you only have an hour a day to work, would it help keep you focused?

Always focus on your initial reason for doing work in the first place.

After all that reason is still there until you reach your goal.

Create a schedule for your day to keep you from getting distracted.

Distractions are everywhere.

It pops up on your phone.

It pops up from people wanting to chat at work.
It pops up in the form of personal problems.
Whatever it may be, distractions are abound.

The only cure is clear concentration.
To have clear concentration it must be something you are excited about.
To have clear knowledge that this action will lead you to something exciting.

If you find the work boring, It will be difficult for you to concentrate too long.
Sometimes it takes reassessing your life and admitting your work is boring for you to consider a change in direction.

Your goal will have more than one path.
Some paths boring, some paths dangerous, some paths redundant, and some paths magical.
You may not know better until you try.
After all the journey is everything.

If reaching your goal takes decades of work that makes you miserable, is it really worth it?
The changes to your personality may be irreversible.

Always keep the goal in mind whilst searching for an enjoyable path to attain it.

After all if you are easily distracted from your goal, then do you really want it?

Ask yourself the hard questions.
Is this something you really want? Or is this something society wants for you?

Many people who appear successful to society are secretly miserable.
Make sure you are aware of every little detail of your life.
Sit down and really decide what will make you happy at the end of your life.

What work will you be really happy to do?
What are the causes and people you would be happy to serve?
How much money you want?
What kind of relationships you want?
If you can build a clear vision of this life for you, distractions will become irrelevant.
Irrelevant because nothing will be able to distract you from your perfect vision.

Is what you are doing right now moving you towards that life?
If not stop, and start doing the things what will.
It really is that simple.

Anyone who is distracted for too long from the task in hand has no business doing that task. They should instead be doing something that makes them happy.

We can't be happy all the time otherwise we wouldn't be able to recognize it.

But distraction is a clear indicator you may not be on the right path for you.

Clearly define your path and distraction will be powerless.

Chapter 24:
Get Motivated Even When You Don't Feel Like It

Have you ever heard of the LOCUS Rule? If you haven't, let me explain it to you. The Locus of control is the aspect of your life in which you come to realize the degree to which you believe you have control over your life and the things revolving around it.

Let's simplify it with an example. Let's say you are presented with a situation where you have to solve a puzzle. When you attempt it, luckily you solve it in record time. Someone comes to you and says that you were able to do it because you are smart.

The next time you are presented with a relatively simpler problem, you spend much more time on it and might not be able to solve some hard ones at all. So you feel demotivated and you don't want to do any more puzzles.

But if you were to spend a considerable time solving the original puzzle while doing calculations and taking educational guesses and thinking a lot. Someone would have pointed out that you are a hard worker, so good Job!

So the next time you would feel more motivated to do any similar job and you might be able to perform better in the next one's.

The first case was determined by an external, unprecedented, immeasurable, God-gifted feat. If at any time, you cannot get something done, you would think that you don't have it in you anymore and you are just a piece of sheer luck.

But if you know for sure that you can achieve absolutely anything, just as you keep doing what you do best, and that being your hard work. Then everything seems achievable and everything seems easy no matter how long it gets.

Life is a balloon stretched over this rule. Life always presents us with opportunities but we miss out on most. We miss out because we have this fear of non-confidence within us. We fear the unknown and so we get stuck in the same old rut of depression, anxiety, and fear.

All these things have a simple initiative for a solution.

You need to be transparent with yourself. You need to prove your strengths and strategies to yourself. And you have to tell it to yourself that you only need a little willpower to always keep one little straw to stick to, for when every support seems to turn to dust.

Look around you. You are still a lot better than the majority. You still have a brain to keep you on your ability to self-analyze.

Think about it. You failed today, but you had some success some time ago. So if you can spend some time feeling sorry for yourself, you can spend the same time trying to put your mind, heart, and body to get up one more time and try one more time.

You might fail again and again and again, but remember that life is not based on one moment of luck. Life is a campaign of hard work followed by dedication and motivation.

Chapter 25:
How To Stop Being A Narcissist

Narcissists often get flak for being incapable of change.

The reason, according to psychologists, is that most narcissists aren't really aware of their narcissistic tendencies. These issues are often deep-seated, and self-preservation stops them from even recognizing their problems.

But chances are, if you're reading this, you're one of those who want to change. Admitting you might have Narcissistic Personality Disorder is already a step forward.

Self-aware narcissists can change. In this article, we've curated seven key steps on how to stop being a narcissist, according to some of the world's top psychology experts. We then go through the negative impacts of narcissism, followed by a discussion on whether narcissists can really change.

You have Narcissistic Personality Disorder if you:

- Think quite highly of yourself, like you're the only important person in the world.
- Are self-entitled and feel that you deserve nothing but the best.
- Demand recognition even if you didn't do anything to deserve it.
- Exaggerate your skills and achievements and brag about them excessively.
- Make everything about you.
- Use and manipulate people to get what you want.

- Unwilling to recognize and value the needs of others.

Overcoming narcissism is no simple process. Absolute change may be near impossible. However, you can make changes that will create a positive impact on your life.

Know what your "triggers" are: Narcissistic behaviour often emerges when a person suffering from Narcissistic Personality Disorder gets "triggered."

According to Greenberg, "triggers" are: "…situations, words, or behaviours that arouse strong negative feelings in you. People with narcissistic issues tend to overreact when they are "triggered" and do things that they later regret."

As a first step, it's important to know in which situations your narcissism comes out. Learning what they are can help you identify the reasons behind your narcissism, so you may be able to handle them accordingly.

For example, if you experience narcissistic tendencies and want to become aware of your triggers, you may notice that you often feel a surge of anger when someone you perceive being of a "lower status" challenges your authority in the workplace

Or you may notice that you are often dismissive of other people when they suggest ideas.

Whatever your particular triggers are, start to take note of them. It may be useful to carry a notebook with you or jot them down in a note-taking app on your phone.

Over time, you'll start to notice patterns on when you feel triggered by others and react with narcissistic tendencies.

Manage your impulses: Narcissist people are often impulsive and make decisions without thinking of the consequences. If you display narcissist tendencies, it's important to emphasize thinking first and reacting later.

According to Greenberg: "Practice inhibiting or delaying your normal response when triggered. Your 'normal' response is the now unwanted one that you do automatically. It has become wired as a habit into the neurons of your brain."

The key step to changing your behaviours is to become aware of your impulses. This gives you the opportunity to create behavioural change in your life.

Taking note of your triggers as recommended in step one will teach you to create some space between the stimulus of the trigger and your response. Pausing when triggered opens up the opportunity to create a new set of behaviours

Chapter 26:
10 Habits of Larry Ellison

Larry Ellison once said that most great achievers are motivated more by fear of failure than success. And, to maintain a successful drive, you must be ready to ditch the conventional way of operating. Larry Ellison, the founder, and CEO of Oracle and a college dropout turned billionaire, is best known for his unconventional way of looking at things. The man was not bothered for supporting Trump even if his fellow tech-moguls had agreed not to.

Larry Ellison dubbed the "flamboyant billionaire," is one of the most admired personalities in the tech world. His urge to always being the winner is what always keeps him ahead of anyone else. So, what is it like to be Larry Ellison?

Here are 10 habits of Larry Ellison.

1. Don't Be Blinded by Conventions

Larry Ellison believes that to thrive in your career or life, you must stray from the typical ways of doing things. He isn't bothered with reinventing the wheel as long as the idea is from his perspective. He dropped out of school several times ideally because he was not a strong supporter of formal education. Still, his desire to learn about computer design persisted until he hit the target.

2. Put Your Ideas Into Action

You must absorb from Larry that the ability to execute ideas better than anyone else is critical to success. He's one person who you will run to with a business idea, and he will exemplify it into a billion-dollar empire. The relational database he invented was not his idea but that of IBM. What he excelled at was turning this concept into a great product, which IBM failed to do.

3. Your Focus Must Be on the Right Product

You could be the most skilled and dedicated entrepreneur in the world, but the ideal mantra for success is neither of the two. Oracle is a firm believer in attracting only the best products. This is why Larry only hires the best engineers who can successfully upgrade software that can sell itself without the need for marketing. Larry understands that if you don't have a great product, yes, you'll get clients, but you will not keep them long enough.

4. Obsess Over Winning

Larry once said that he is hooked to always being the first because the moment you start winning, you become addicted to it. His vicious competitive drive is so obvious considering that he's inspired by Genghis Khan, who desired to triumph at the expense of others. However, Larry's hungry mind is more concerned with being first in the competition than with money. It is wise that you get to the peak quicker than others, but only with self-consciousness.

5. Growth Is Continuous

Larry's vocabulary does not include the words "retirement," as he is a person who never stops growing. At the age of 70, he retired from Oracle and joined Tesla's board of directors. Along with the latter position, he launched a Sensei company, which focuses on indoor food production. He emphasizes that if you want to make a career in business, you must constantly reinvent yourself.

6. A Degree Is Not Mandatory for Success

Most of the billionaires at Silicon Valley can attest to succeeding even if you lack formal qualifications. Once you realize what you're passionate about, work towards sharpening those strengths. Once Larry realized that he was into computer designs, he only stayed in school long enough to learn about it. Moreover, his reading habits continued, which is how he invented the relational database.

7. Make the Tough Choices

When you are building a company or leading an organization, you will have to make difficult decisions to ensure long-term benefits. Larry, in the 90s, decided to let go an entire management team, which according to him, was the toughest decision ever since those people had been with the company for decades. He believed that someone with the ability to run a $15 million company could not necessarily run a $1 billion company.

8. Expect Professionalism

As soon as you walk into the Oracle office, expectations are that you're professional in your demeanor. And if you fail to, count your future with the company over. At Oracle, contrary to Silicon Valley, all programmers are expected to dress professionally in formal attire.

9. Always Remember To Give Back

Most wealthy people are also known for their charitable gestures, and Larry is one of them. Although he doesn't talk much about his charitable contributions, he supports medical research and green energy. Alongside the healthy benefits, volunteering gives you a sense of purpose in society.

10. Nerds Can Be Bad Boys or Superheroes

If you're yet convinced, here is some tea. Larry Ellison is considered an iconic "bad boy" who dates models, explores daring adventures like racing fast autos, and ends up in surgery for injuries sustained. More to it, he was the inspiration for Robert Downey Jr.'s Tony Stark, the bad boy billionaire in the "Iron Man" films, according to CNBC.

Conclusion

One of the ideal ways of improving your life is by emulating from the best. Larry Ellison is a superb investor and entrepreneur who deserves your attention. Learn from his habits and see how they affect your life.

Chapter 27:
Treat Failure Like A Scientist

Have you ever studied the life of a scientist in general? Do you know what a scientist actually does? A scientist conducts experiments to study the true nature and the working of the universe.

Scientists have a strategy to work ahead. They perform the experiments and they get results. Some are in the favor of their original theory and some are against them.

But never do these results have a personal attachment to anything. The results are data points and each data point has an importance to the study.

The scientist cannot neglect any result whether it be a success or a total failure because it will make them realize the faults they made the first time and will eventually help them and others after them to take a better start or a better theory.

The same is the case with our lives. We have to understand the working philosophy of life and failures.

People get carried away with the smallest of setbacks. We get discouraged and demotivated by the smallest of things that might not even be that big a deal. But we are so used to making such a big deal out of every little hitch.

We get stuck in the pitfall that we create ourselves and never try to realize the true mercy or lesson that little moments of pain and failure might have taught us.

Failures leave a mark, that is for sure. But those marks don't have to be bad. Whether you make those marks a war wound or a scar is up to you.

You live life as you please. Other people do the same thing. But we are not all the same, and no one can say what is right and what is wrong. But there is a simple way to judge. Let's say we get a reward for doing something good and it makes us feel good.

But when we do something from the top of our head and we are not sure what impact it will have on others, the result will make it clear and will be a lesson for the rest of our lives.

Your intentions are always in the right place, but failures still get you. So failing is not fun, but it should be held against you. You had a reason for all of this and now you have a reason to not do the same thing again.

This result made you eliminate one small thing that made you look bad the first time. So you were able to remove one more spot from your bigger picture and now you are a better individual altogether.

Failure is simply a cost you have to pay on the way to being right. Your failures don't define you, but you can define your failures. You can either let it remain a failure or you can change it into a success story by sticking to the process of turning wrongs into rights. And you will go through this learning throughout your life.

Chapter 28:
Happy People Choose to Exercise

There is a feeling you get when you just finish your workout, and you feel amazing, much better than you were feeling before. Even when you are not feeling motivated to go to the gym, just thinking about this feeling makes you get up, leave your bed and get going to the gym. This feeling can also be called an endorphin rush. Exercise indeed makes you happier in multiple ways.

Firstly, movement helps you bond with others that are in the brain chemistry of it all. Your heart rate is going up, you are using your body, engaging your muscles, your brain chemistry will change, and it will make it easier for you to connect and bond with other people. It also changes how your trust people. Research also showed that social pressures like a hug, laughing, or high-five are also enhanced. You will also find your new fitness fam, the people you will be working out with, and because you will have a shared interest that is having a healthy lifestyle will help you have a stronger bond with them. And as experts say that having strong relationships and connections in life will help you in overall happiness.

We have already discussed those exercise increases endorphins but what you do not know is that it increases a lot more brain chemicals that make you feel happy and good about yourself. Some of the brain chemicals that increase are; dopamine, endorphins, endocannabinoid and adrenaline. All of these chemicals are associated with feeling confident, capable, and happy. The amount of stress, physical pain, and anxiety also decrease significantly. A chemical that your body creates when your muscles contract is called "myokine", it is also shown to boost happiness and relieve stress.

Secondly, exercise can help boost your confidence, and of course, when it comes to feeling empowered and happy, confidence is the key. "At the point when you move with others, it's anything but a solid feeling of 'greater than self' probability that causes individuals to feel more idealistic and enabled, "Also, it permits individuals to feel more engaged turning around the difficulties in their own lives. What's more, that is a fascinating side advantage of moving with others because there's an encapsulated feeling of 'we're in the same boat' that converts into self-assurance and the capacity to take on difficulties in your day; to day existence."

Thirdly, exercising outdoors affects your brain, similar to meditation. In case you're similar to the innumerable other people who have found out about the advantages of contemplation yet can't make the time, uplifting news. You may not need to contemplate to get a portion of the advantages. Researchers found that exercising outside can similarly affect the cerebrum and disposition as reflection. Exercising outside immediately affects a state of mind that is amazingly incredible for wretchedness and nervousness. Since it's anything but a state in your mind that is the same as contemplation, the condition of open mindfulness,"

Chapter 29:
4 Ways to Deal with Feelings of Inferiority When Comparing to Others

When we're feeling inferior, it's usually a result of comparing ourselves to other people and feeling like we don't measure up. And let's be real, it happens all. The. Damn. Time. You could be scrolling through your Instagram feed, notice a new picture of someone you follow, and think: *Wow, how do they always look so perfect?! No amount of filters will make me look like that!* Or maybe you show up to a party, and you quickly realize you're in a room full of accomplished people with exciting lives, and the thought of introducing yourself sends you into a panic. Suddenly, you're glancing at the door and wondering what your best escape plan is. You could be meeting your partner's family for the first time, and you're worried that you won't fit in or that they'll think you're not good enough. You might feel easily intimidated by other people and constantly obsess over what they think of you, even though it's beyond your control.

Don't worry! We have some coping strategies for you that will help you work through your feelings. Try 'em out and see for yourself!

1. Engage in compassionate self-talk
When we feel inferior, we tend to pick ourselves apart and be hard on ourselves. Don't fall into the trap of being your own worst critic! Instead, build your <u>self-confidence</u> and self-esteem by saying positive things to yourself that resonate with you: *I'm feeling inferior right now, but I know my*

worth. *I'm not defined by my credentials, my possessions, or my appearance. I am whole.*

2. Reach out for support or connect with a friend

Just like the Beatles song goes: *I get by with a little help from my friends!* Reach out to someone you can trust and who will be there for you. You might feel inferior now, but it doesn't mean you have to navigate it alone! Get all of those negative feelings off your chest. Having someone there to validate our feelings can be so helpful!

3. Give yourself a pep talk and utilize a helpful statement

Comparing ourselves to other people just brings down our mood and makes us feel like garbage. Sometimes, we gotta give ourselves a little pep talk to turn those negative thoughts around. *I feel inferior right now, but I can get through this! I'm not the only person who has felt this way, and I won't be the last. Everything is gonna be okay!*

4. Comfort yourself like a friend

If you don't have anyone who can be there for you at this moment, that's okay. You can be there for yourself! Think about how you would want a loved one to comfort you at this moment. Pat yourself on the back, treat yourself to some junk food, cuddle up on the couch with a warm, fuzzy blanket and binge your favorite show on Netflix. Be the friend you need right now!

Chapter 30:
How To Deal With Uncertainty?

How many of you are going through life right now but are dealing with a load of uncertainty that is weighing heavily on your mind?

You could be worrying about your career or work related matters: you wonder because the economy is taking a hit, whether you will still have your job tomorrow, whether your business would survive, or even if the economy is good, you are uncertain if you quit the current job you hate whether you are able to find another job in the near future or if you will even be competent in your new profession.

Or you could be worrying about your loved ones, your child who is studying overseas, or your spouse where they are working in the healthcare profession, working in the police or fire department, or even the military, where their lives are put at risk every single day, you worry if there will be one day that you might lose them and they won't come home.

Or you could be uncertain about smaller matters, matters such as if your date went well and if they would give you a call to ask you out again.

Whatever these may be, they all fall under the umbrella of uncertainty.

I would like to share with you uncertainties I faced personally and I would like to provide you with action steps to deal with them.

Recently I had been struggling with many uncertainties in my life. While they might not be your struggles I believe I would be able to provide more value if i shared my own story.

The first uncertainty I had was that I had recently restarted my publishing business after being away from it for a year, I was so afraid of what the market condition was like now, I was afraid of the competition, I was afraid I would fail again. I was afraid I would waste more of my time building up a business only to have it taken away from me.

The second worry I had was that I had also just begun taking my real estate exam to become a licensed realtor. I started having doubts about myself that I would ever become a competent realtor like my peers and I would look like a fool and I would feel disappointed with myself thereafter.

The next uncertainty I had was whether I would get the jobs that I applied for. I had decided to take on a part or full-time position to grow my professional career and I was afraid Whether the hours I spent on job applications would be in vain and that i would get no responses or even worse, rejections.

The final uncertainty was with stocks. Due to the incredible market volatility, I couldn't sleep properly every night because I wasn't sure what was gonna happen tmr. Whether I was gonna lose money while i was asleep.

I went about days with all these negative thoughts looming in my mind. It affected my sleep, my well-being, and my happiness. I started becoming dreary, unhappy, and lifeless. I spent 80% of my waking hours with these fears and doubts, and constantly beating myself up for feeling this way and it only made matters worse.

One day I decided it was enough. I took a deep breath and started collecting myself. I had had enough and I was so done with feeling these uncertainty and feeling sorry for myself.

I made the decision to accept my struggles, that they were a part of life and that there was no point in worrying about it. I decided it that I would just work hard on these areas, keep doing my best, and that whatever outcomes doesn't matter because I've given it my all. And finally I decided to live my day to the fullest and just be grateful that I even get to have the opportunity to pursue these ventures. After going through this process day in and day out, I became more at peace with myself. I started feeling less anxiety and adopted a more optimistic and positive mindset.

Here's what I realized. Uncertainty is born out of fear. This could be fear of losing someone, fear of the unknown, or even fear of failure. I had immense fears of failure that it crippled me to a really low point in my life. And the only way to overcome fear is first to accept that it is normal to be fearful, and then after to not let that fear get in the way of your happiness because life is too short for you to spend in a state of fearfulness. Rather, spend your time feeling grateful for your life and just try your best in everything that you do. Keep working on your dreams as if it were your last day on this earth, keep loving your spouse or child as though it was their last day on this earth, and ask yourself, is this how you would want to spend your time letting fear and uncertainty feed on your happiness? Or would you rather cherish every single moment you have with yourself and your family, and to live life with abundance instead.

This is my challenge to you. Uncertainty can only cripple you if you let it. Focus on your journey, your path, and trust in the process. But most importantly, Trust in yourself, believe in yourself even if no one else will. You owe that much love and compassion to yourself. I know you can do it.

Chapter 31:

Happy People Give Freely

"For it is in giving that we receive." - Saint Francis of Assisi.

A Chinese saying goes by, "If you want happiness for an hour, take a nap. If you want happiness for a day, go fishing. If you want happiness for a year, inherit a fortune. If you want happiness for a lifetime, help somebody." It is indeed better to give than to receive. Scientific research provides compelling anecdotal evidence that giving is a powerful pathway to personal growth and lasting happiness. When we give freely, our brain stimulates endorphins and blesses us with a feeling of euphoria. Altruism is hardwired in our brains and tends to provide us with pleasure. Helping others is a secret to living a happier and healthier, wealthier, productive, and more meaningful life.

Whether it's a charity, a piece of advice, a helping hand of any sort, or supporting someone throughout their journey, researchers Dunn, Aknin, Akin, and Norton performed a study. They showed that there is, in fact, a link between generosity and happier life. The gesture of caring about other people and doing something to improve their quality of life is the source of happiness. Once you start giving, you will feel more content and happier, and there will be no going back. You will get addicted to helping others and to the feeling that follows.

A group of psychologists from the University of California Santa Barbara conducted a study to ascertain if generosity is part of human nature. The observation showed that being a giver is more fulfilling than being a receiver and that generosity is deeply embedded in our systems. "You don't need to become a self-sacrificing martyr to feel happier. Just being a little more generous will suffice," says Prof. Tobler.

High-generosity respondents appeared not only happier but happier more often. This overarching sense of happiness in high-generosity individuals may positively affect their higher likelihood of finding life more meaningful. They were also 20% more likely to be optimistic about their future, be proud of themselves, and find enjoyment in their jobs. It's no secret that you have to give a little to get a little. The more generous you are too loved ones, acquaintances, or even strangers, the more likely those selfless deeds will be reciprocated sometime down the line. Neuroeconomics found in a recent study that merely promising to be more generous is enough to trigger a change in our brain that will eventually make us happier.

In a 2006 study, Jorge Moll and colleagues at the National Institutes of Health found that when people give, it could be anything; it activates the warm glow effect, regions of the brain associated with pleasure, social connection, and trust. Whatever you are giving to people, society, or nature, you will find yourself benefiting from a hefty dose of happiness in the process. When you express your gratitude in words or actions, you not only boost your positivity but other people's as well. The more we give, the more we stand to gain purpose, meaning, and happiness – all of the things we look for in life but are so hard to find.

Chapter 32:
How To Develop An Incredible Work Ethic

We've all been there. That feeling of really, really not wanting to go into the office of a morning. It cripples productivity, raises stress levels, and makes us unhappy.

Why Do We Do It To Ourselves?

Unless it stems from deeper issues, the feeling of not wanting to go to work is often the result of a poor work ethic. If you've experienced it yourself recently, that doesn't make you a bad person or employee. A poor work ethic usually arrives subconsciously and is something you'll have little control over or forewarning of its impending arrival.

Thankfully, there are some methods you can employ to improve your work ethic dramatically, and they're not quite as tricky as you might think. To help you get out of that rut and back, fighting fit for a productive time in the office, we've decided to list our top eight tips for improving your work ethic.

1. Start With Your Body – Treat It Right

A healthy body will help you build a healthy approach to work because the two are intrinsically linked.

If you feel lethargic in the morning, the last thing you're going to want to do is to spring out of bed and head to the office. You're far more likely to continually hit the 'snooze' button and curse the fact you even have a job.

Lethargy can be a result of not enough sleep and poor levels of exercise. Therefore if the feeling just described is something you're all too familiar with, it's time to go on something of a permanent health kick. And that doesn't mean ditching all the treats that make you happy – just the process of regularly exercising and eating more healthily.

Walk when you'd normally take the car and swap those regular naughty treats for fruit and glasses of water – you'll be surprised how much more up for it you'll feel each morning.

2. Eliminate As Many Distractions As Possible

How many times do you check your email each day? What about social media? Is your facebook feed something you access every five minutes to check in on what your friends and family are up to?

We live in a world full of distractions. Multiple forms of content, relentless notifications and devices capable of connecting us immediately to the internet are everywhere and seemingly impossible to drag yourself away from.

That's true – unless you can call on your reserves of willpower. Distractions will divert your attention from what matters, and ensure that you have a limited focus on work tasks. In turn, that'll reduce your emotional connection with the business and negatively impact your work ethic.

Check your email only two or three times a day, turn off notifications and leave social media for the moments when you're sat on the sofa with nothing better to do.

3. Measure Your Ethic Against Others

If you're forever cursing your colleague's ability to practically skip into work ready for the day ahead, why not measure your performance against theirs?

Something is different. It might be their mindset, attitude towards their role or lifestyle, but if you can be brave enough to measure your performance against others, you'll quickly suss out where you need to improve.

This can extend far beyond work colleagues, too. For example, if your partner appears to be having the time of their life at work, yet you can barely muster the strength to log onto your computer for the first time each morning, ask them how they're doing it. You never know – you might just learn a thing or two.

Unless you're particularly spritely in the morning, it's unlikely that you'll jump out of bed and head to work full of an endless supply of energy. Still, if you follow our tips above, you'll greatly increase your ability to foster a healthy approach to work. Whenever you feel uninspired by your role, but you know it's something more superficial than job dissatisfaction, check that you're doing all you can to improve your work ethic. As we've demonstrated today, it isn't that difficult at all.

Chapter 33:
Resist Temptations For Success

We all have hopes and dreams. We have a rough sketch of what we want to become and what we want to achieve. Most of us have good intentions for those things too.

But the reality is that process of achieving those things isn't always as simple as we all anticipate. It is all mixed up with all these temptations that are equally alluring and want us to give up everything else for just a moment and enjoy what we are about to indulge in.

You see if you were to make a milestone for a week where you were to lose a pound of weight with rigorous cardio and hours of strict training followed by a strict diet plan. You can't say you won't be tempted by the smell of fries and fried chicken whenever you walk past one.

Surely you would be OK, only if you resisted it and kept walking your way. But if you were to pick up one piece and put it in your mouth, you just destroyed the whole mantra of self-control and self-discipline.

Self-discipline is not just putting your life on track and following a timetable. Self-discipline is not punishing yourself for any mistake. Self-discipline is following a course of actions that will take you to your ultimate goal.

We all are susceptible to weaknesses. We often end up acting against the things and goals that we value the most.

Temptations are nature's way of testing us. It is a test to evaluate our core values and our integrity. It is a litmus test to pick the leaders out of a faction. Temptations are a way of self-analyzing ourselves whether we are worthy enough or are we still distracted with all the shiny things lying around.

It is easy to get a good grade with a little help from here and there. It is easy to follow someone else's path rather than carving our own. It is easier to fake some lab results to be enrolled into a team of representatives.

But when we get the chance to do those things in real life without any outside help on an open stage where the world is judging us, we cannot get ourselves to do any of those things because we cheated n the first place and never engaged the creative factory of our mind.

So how should you approach this problem? It is a simple step-by-step process.

Start by removing the temptations. Check for any loopholes in your environment and kick them out to keep them away long enough till you are more in control.

Next, you need to take some time to think about your way of thinking as an unbiased and nonhuman object. Try to find the flaws and reinvent them to disengage any magnets in your personality that keep attracting you to those temptations.

Last but not the least, put a zipper on your pocket and control your spending habits and you will get away from any unnecessary temptation leading you to a better successful life!

Chapter 34:
The Magic of Journaling

Today we're going to talk about the power of journaling, and why you should start making it as part of your daily habit starting today.

Everyday, every second of our lives, we are bombarded with things coming at our way. From our colleagues, our bosses, to our friends, families, relationships, and most importantly, ourselves. Life gets hectic and crazy sometimes. We have a million things racing through our minds and we don't have the time or place to let it all out so we keep it bottled up inside.

This creates a backlog of emotions, feelings, things, that we leave undealt with. We start to miss the little details along the way, or our mood gets affected because we can't seem to get rid of the negativity festering up inside of us. If we don't have anyone readily available to talk to us, these feelings that have been building inside of us could end up spilling over and affecting our performance at the workplace, at home, whatever it may be.

We are not able to perform these roles at home or at work effectively as a result. This is where the power of journaling comes into play.

Journaling is such an important tool for us to put into paper or into words every single emotion that we are feeling. Every thought that we are thinking. And this works sort of like a cleanse. We are cleansing, decluttering, and unpacking all the things that are jumbled up in our head. By writing these feelings down, we are not only able to keep a clear head, but it also gives us a reference point to come back to if there are any unresolved problems that we feel we need to work on at a later date.

Journaling has worked wonders for me. I've never thought it to be a habit work incorporating into my life because i thought hey, it's another thing for me to do on top of my already hectic day. I don't have time for this. Basically giving 1001 reasons not to do it.

But I came across this life coach that described the wonders of journaling as I am describing to you right now. And I thought. Why not just give it a try.

I did. And it changed my life.

I never realized how powerful journaling could actually be in transforming my state of mind and to always keep me grounded and focused. Everytime I felt that i was distracted, had something I couldn't work through in my mind, I would pick up my ipad and start typing it down in a journal app.

With technology, it has made journaling a much more enjoyable experience for me and one that i can simply do on the fly, anywhere, anytime. I didn't have to fumble around to find my pen and book, i just opened up the app and started typing away every single feeling and thought.

Journaling helped me see the big picture. It helped me become more aware of the things that are working for me and things that aren't. I was able to focus more on the areas that were bringing more joy in my life and to eliminate the situations and activities that were draining me of my energy and spirit.

Journaling can be anything you want it to be. There are no fixed rules as to how you must journal. Just write whatever comes to your mind. You will be surprised by how much you can learn from yourself. Many a times we forget that we are our best teacher. Other people can't learn our lessons for us, only we can.

So next time you feel sluggish, depressed, unhappy, or even ecstatic and over the moon, write down how and why you got to that place. No judgement, no berating yourself, just pouring your heart and soul onto a piece of paper or into a journaling app. I'll be looking forward to hearing of your transformation from the power of journaling.

Chapter 35:
How To Let Your Values Drive Your Choices

Nearly every problem you face is temporary. But these temporary problems cause immediate pain. And we often let this pain drive our choices and actions.

For example…

An employee suffering from the pain of not feeling important enough or powerful enough might take a terrible job with a fancy title…and so on. This is how you make choices you wouldn't normally make. When you let the problem drive your decisions, you make exceptions and "just this once" choices to resolve the pain, annoyance, or uncertainty that you're feeling in the moment.

How can we avoid this pitfall and make better long-term choices while still resolving short-term pain?

Here's an approach I've been trying recently. See if it works for you

One of the solutions I've been trying out is to let my values drive my choices. That doesn't mean I ignore other aspects of my decision-making process. I simply add my core values into the mix.

For example, if I'm working on a problem in my business, rather than just asking, "Will this make money?"

I can ask, "Is this in alignment with my values?" And then, "Will this make money?"

If I say no to either, then I look for another option.

The idea behind this method is that if we live and work in alignment with our values, we're more likely to live a life we are proud of rather than one we regret.

THE POWER OF A CONSTRAINT YOU BELIEVE IN

Every decision is made within some type of constraint. Maybe it's how much knowledge you have. Maybe it's how much money you have. Maybe it's how many resources you have. Why not what values you have? Making better choices is often a matter of choosing better constraints. By limiting your options to those that fit your values, you are taking an important step to ensuring that your behavior matches your beliefs. (Plus, constraints will boost your creativity.)

Know your principles, and you can choose your methods.

HOW TO PUT THIS INTO PRACTICE

Most people never take the time to think about their values, write them down, and clarify them. Maybe it sounds too simple or unnecessary.

My 2014 Integrity Report was the first time I sat down to clarify my values and tie them directly to my work.

You are welcome to use that report as a template for discovering your values and aligning them with your work and life.

THE BOTTOM LINE

If you never sit down to think about your values, then you'll be more likely to make decisions based on whatever information is in front of you at the time. That can be a recipe for regret down the road.

Life is complex, and we are all faced with moments in our personal and professional lives that require us to choose without as much information as we need. The default assumption is that we need more knowledge or research in these situations, but often we just need a clear understanding of our values.

Chapter 36:
How Smart Do You Have To Be To Succeed

How smart do you have to be to succeed? How intelligent do you need to be to become a successful entrepreneur? How well does your training program need to be to become an elite athlete? How perfect does your weight loss program need to be to burn fat?

We don't often ask ourselves questions, but they are built into our beliefs and actions about many phases of life. We often think that we aren't succeeding because we haven't found the right strategy or because we weren't born with the right talents. Perhaps that is true. Or, perhaps there is an untold side of the story.

THRESHOLD THEORY

The surprising discovery that came out of Terman's study is best described by creativity researcher and physician Nancy Andreasen as Threshold Theory…

"Although many people continue to equate intelligence with genius, a crucial conclusion from Terman's study is that having a high IQ is not equivalent to being highly creative. Subsequent studies by other researchers have reinforced Terman's conclusions, leading to what's known as the threshold theory, which holds that above a certain level, intelligence doesn't have much effect on creativity: most creative people are pretty smart,

but they don't have to be that smart, at least as measured by conventional intelligence tests. An IQ of 120, indicating that someone is very smart but not exceptionally so, is generally considered sufficient for creative genius."

THRESHOLD THEORY IN EVERYDAY LIFE

If you look around, you'll see that the Threshold Theory applies to many things in life. There is a minimum threshold of competence that you need to develop in nearly any endeavor. Success is rarely as simple as "just work harder."

Beyond that threshold, however, the difference is between those who put in the work and those who get distracted. Once you have a basic grasp of the right things to do, it becomes about the consistency of doing the right things more often. Once you understand the fundamentals, it comes down to your habits.

WRITING

Assuming you understand the core principles of writing and the basics of grammar, what determines your ability to write well more than anything else is writing a lot. Once you reach the threshold of writing a decent sentence, the thing that leads to success is writing more.

ENTREPRENEURSHIP

Assuming you know what the most important metric is for your business, what makes the biggest difference is focusing on that metric every day. Once you cross the basic threshold of knowing what to work on, the most important thing is continuing to work on that one thing and not something else.

If you're brand new to an area, then it's possible you haven't learned enough to cross the threshold yet. But for most of us, we know what works, and we have enough knowledge to make progress. It's not about being more intelligent or more skilled, and it's about overcoming distraction and doing the work that already works.

www.ingramcontent.com/pod-product-compliance
Lightning Source LLC
Chambersburg PA
CBHW070923080526
44589CB00013B/1410